Great Quicksolve Whodunit Puzzles

MINI-MYSTERIES FOR YOU TO SOLVE

Jim Sukach
Illustrated by Lucy Corvino

D0042989

Sterling Publishing Co., Inc.
New York

To my mother, Marguerite Sukach

Library of Congress Cataloging-in-Publication Data

Sukach, Jim.
    Great Quicksolve whodunit puzzles / Jim Sukach ; illustrated
by Lucy Corvino.
        p. cm.
    Includes index.
    ISBN 0-8069-3827-7
    1. Puzzles. 2. Detective and mystery stories. 3. Literary
recreations. I. Title.
GV1507.D4S826   1998
793.73—dc21   97-43671
                                                                                  CIP

10   9   8   7   6   5   4   3   2

First paperback edition published in 1999 by
Sterling Publishing Company, Inc.
387 Park Avenue South, New York, N.Y. 10016
© 1998 by James Richard Sukach
Distributed in Canada by Sterling Publishing
% Canadian Manda Group, One Atlantic Avenue, Suite 105
Toronto, Ontario, Canada M6K 3E7
Distributed in Great Britain and Europe by Chris Lloyd
463 Ashley Road, Parkstone Poole, Dorset BH14 0AX, England
Distributed in Australia by Capricorn Link (Australia) Pty Ltd.
P.O. Box 6651, Baulkham Hills, Business Centre, NSW 2153, Australia
Printed in China

Sterling ISBN 0-8069-3827-7 Trade
                0-8069-4251-7 Paper

Contents

• • • • • • • • •

Dr. J.L. Quicksolve

• • • • • • • • •

Dr. Jeffrey Lynn Quicksolve, professor of criminology, retired from the police force as a detective at a very young age. Now he works with various police agencies and private detectives as a consultant when he is not teaching at the university.

He certainly knows his business, solving crimes. Many people are amazed at how he solves so many crimes so quickly. He says, "The more you know about people and the world we live in, the easier it is to solve a problem."

His son, Junior, enjoys learning too, and he solves a few mysteries himself.

Read, listen, think carefully, and you can solve these crimes too!

Foul Play

• • • • • • • •

Sergeant Rebekah Shurshot wondered if it bothered her more when the murder scene was a spooky place like a dark woods or a railroad yard, or a comfortable and cozy-looking place like this living room in a warm suburban home. She, Dr. J.L. Quicksolve, and Lieutenant Rootumout looked down at the body of Calvin Callumwright. The body lay on its back. The arms were crossed over his chest as if a mortician had positioned them for a funeral. The left hand made a fist, and the right lay across the wrist as if grasping it. It looked staged to Sergeant Shurshot. "Maybe he was killed somewhere else and brought here," she said to Lieutenant Rootumout.

"There's no sign the body was moved," he said.

"Any suspects?" Dr. Quicksolve asked as he looked around the room. He noticed an over-turned lamp, and a chair had been pushed out of place.

"We have reports that two local football heroes, Hal Holden and Pierce Fumble, were in a local bar a few hours ago. They both were threatening to do something about the way Calvin Callum-wright refereed this afternoon's football game. Apparently, they lost the championship game on several close calls," Lieutenant Rootumout said.

"Did they leave together?" Sergeant Shurshot asked.

"No. Hal left around 10 P.M. Pierce left about an hour later," Lieutenant Rootumout said.

"We had better find both of them right away and bring them in for questioning," Sergeant Shurshot suggested.

"Callumwright has made his last call," Lieutenant Rootumout said.

"And, of course, he has named our suspect," Dr. Quicksolve added.

What is Dr. Quicksolve talking about?

Solution on page 88.

Maps and Treats

•••••••••

Junior was glad to be visiting Grandma and Grandpa Quicksolve, especially when his twin cousins, Flora and Fauna, were there too. But he was disappointed the first night when Grandpa said he was leaving in the morning and would be out of town for four days. "What will we do without you?" Flora asked Grandpa.

He just said, "You'll see."

The next morning Junior was up first, as usual, and found the note Grandpa had left. It said, "Here's something for you to do for the next four days. Follow the directions and keep a good record of what you do. There will be a small surprise each day and a big one when I get back if you do a good job. Have fun! Grandpa."

The first day's directions led the trio across the countryside through pasture land and orchards. The directions said, "Start at the well. Walk one-half mile southeast. Go one-half mile northeast. Go one-half mile southeast. Go one-half mile northeast. Eat lunch."

After traipsing over hill and dale, they were glad to find the first prize, a picnic basket full of sandwiches, lemonade, and Grandma's famous chocolate chip cookies.

The second day's directions said, "Start at Main and Maple in town. Go east one block; north one block; west one block; south two blocks; and east

one block. Flora and Fauna enjoyed the window shopping as they walked through town. They were impressed with Junior's patience as he walked along, trying to figure out the secret reason Grandpa had for sending them marching around town. The day's prize was Grandma waiting in front of the ice cream shop to buy them all a treat.

The third day's directions were simple, but Grandma had to drive them. The directions said, "Go south one mile. Go east one-half mile." They ended up at Grandma and Grandpa's friends' farm, where they rode horses for hours while Grandma visited.

The fourth day's directions said, "Start where

you were and do it again." They figured out that meant go south one mile and east one-half mile from where they were the day before. That took them to the lake, where they swam and picnicked all day.

"But what's the final surprise?" Flora asked.

"I've been making maps, and I think I know where to look," Junior said. He showed the girls the maps.

"Let's go!" Fauna said.

Where did they go?

Solution on page 87.

Pie

• • • • • • • • •

Junior sat at the dining room table proudly show-ing Flora and Fauna how he could use his finger-print kit to identify fingerprints that were on the glass he held. Grandma Quicksolve was mopping the kitchen floor after an evening of baking pies. "The kitchen floor is wet, and the pies are still cooling. We will wait until everyone is up in the morning and have pie together," Grandma said. The girls had gotten ready for bed, hoping to have pie before they went to sleep. They were disap-pointed.

"But Grandpa gets up late," Flora protested.

"We can't wait," said Fauna.

"We will wait," Grandma said with a tone that indicated the conversation was over. Junior finished his demonstration, and everyone went to bed.

Junior got up early the next morning. He sat at the dining room table and waited for the others. He could see across the kitchen where one of Grandma's pies had been cut. One piece was gone. Grandma would be upset.

Flora came downstairs still barefoot and in her pajamas. She sat next to Junior, who pointed to the pies, just as Fauna came into the dining room dressed like her sister.

"Someone had a piece of pie," Junior said.

"But who?" Flora challenged.

"I'll get my fingerprint kit," Junior said.

"Don't you think a smart crook would wear gloves or wipe off the fingerprints?" Flora asked.

"Especially when he..." Fauna said.

"Or she..." Flora interrupted.

"Knows you have a fingerprint kit," Fauna said.

"I guess neither of you would have left fingerprints after my demonstration," Junior said. "But I do think one of you came downstairs last night and had a piece of pie. It won't be hard for me to figure out which one of you did it."

How can Junior tell who took the piece of pie?

Solution on page 95.

A Ride with Grandma

• • • • • • • • •

Grandma Quicksolve was a typical grandmother
in the kitchen, where she loved to bake cakes and
pies. When she got to the garage, it was a different story. Here she became a self-described "radi-
cal girl." When she got behind the wheel of her
fire-engine red Mustang convertible, she liked to
cook in a very different way. "Oops!" she said, as
if she did not intend to fishtail out of the farm-
yard and onto the road, throwing gravel until the
tires spun and smoked across the blacktop. She
did not want to be a bad influence on her grand-
children. Junior rode in the front seat and Flora
and Fauna rode in the back. The twins' ponytails

blew out straight in the wind. All four faces had matching grins.

"There's Bobbi's house," Flora said as they passed a farm with four large apple trees standing in the front yard. They were loaded with bright red apples. The twins bent their heads together, whispering.

"You'll never guess how many kinds of apples they grow in their front yard!" Fauna said to Junior, shouting to be heard over the rushing wind.

"You're right about that!" Junior said.

Disappointed, Fauna said, "Take a guess!"

"Couldn't guess!" Junior said.

"There are four trees!" Flora said, encouraging Junior to pick a number. Both girls were frustrated at Junior's reluctance.

Finally, Junior said, "There are seven kinds of apples! But, of course, I could never guess!"

Flora and Fauna turned to each other with surprised looks. "How did you guess?" Flora asked.

"Grandpa told me," Junior confessed. "I could never guess!"

Why did Junior keep insisting he couldn't guess?
How could the answer be seven when there are four trees?

Solution on page 89.

Sick Trick

• • • • • • • • •

Junior sat at Grandma Quicksolve's kitchen table finishing the hot dog he had cooked as a snack. He decided it was delicious with mustard and onions. He had been disappointed at first because he couldn't find any ketchup in Grandma's refrigerator.

Just as he put a bite of hot dog into his mouth,

Flora came into the house supporting Fauna, who had a thick turban of bandages covering her head. Large spots of red soaked through the mass of white. Thick red drops dripped down to her nose and the corners of her mouth. One leg was similarly bandaged with a large red spot and red drops running down from the bandaged area. Fauna grimaced and whimpered with each step.

"Fauna's been hurt!" Flora said.

Junior stood up in surprise. "What happened?" he asked.

"She was riding her bike down the street just in front of the school when a speeding car hit her head-on! She has amnesia!" Flora said.

"Woof! Woof!" Fauna said suddenly.

"She thinks she's a dog!" Flora said.

Fauna stuck out her tongue and began to pant.

"Ha!" Junior laughed.

"She's hurt!" Flora said.

"Ha! Ha!" Junior continued laughing.

"How can you laugh?" Flora asked her cousin.

"Woof! Woof!" Fauna said faintly.

"You are both sick!" Junior said, unable to stop laughing. "I don't believe this!"

Why didn't Junior believe Fauna had been in an accident?

Solution on page 90.

Country Killing

• • • • • • • •

Dr. J.L. Quicksolve sped along in his bright yellow VW Beetle. He looked at the sun beginning to set to his right across the expanse of corn growing in the fields. Sun and corn belong together, he thought, out here in this beautiful country atmosphere—but not murder.

Sergeant Rebekah Shurshot met Dr. Quicksolve at the door of the small house nestled between the huge oak trees, a small oasis in the sea of cornfields. The front door, hanging to the floor from one hinge, was the first sign something was amiss. The second was the blanket-covered body on the floor. Dr. Quicksolve had to step around it.

Sergeant Shurshot led him through the mass of overturned furniture and broken lamps into the small dining area. Sergeant Shurshot introduced Dr. Quicksolve to Spinner Webb, the nephew of the deceased.

"My aunt had not been feeling well," Spinner said. "She had been depressed ever since her dog, Spookum, disappeared." Dr. Quicksolve noticed the curtains were drawn, as if the elderly lady had wanted to live in the misery of darkness while she mourned. "She didn't answer when I knocked," Mr. Webb continued. "I pushed on the door. It opened barely an inch, stopped by the chain lock. I shouted for her, but I got no answer. I could see inside enough to tell the house had been ransacked. I was worried, so I slammed my shoulder against the door and broke in. I came inside and looked around. I stumbled over my aunt's body in the dark. That scared me half to death!"

"There is one window open in the back," Sergeant Shurshot said. "The screen has been cut."

"The murderer must have escaped through that window," Webb said.

"You weave quite a story, Mr. Webb," Dr. Quicksolve said.

Why did Dr. Quicksolve doubt Spinner Webb's story?

Solution on page 87.

Mary Contrary

• • • • • • • •

Dr. J.L. Quicksolve stood in front of a small sub-urban house with a neatly trimmed lawn. He watched as the seat of the sedan in the driveway was moved forward in order to remove the body wedged between the front and back seat. It was the body of Tim Contrary—recently married, recently deceased.

Inside the house Lieutenant Rootumout was questioning Tim's new bride, Mary. When Dr. Quicksolve entered, the Lieutenant paused and summarized what he had learned so far. He explained that Mr. Contrary's body was discov-ered in the back seat of Mr. Contrary's car that morning by Phyllis, their mail carrier. Mary said she and her husband had had an argument the previous night around 11 o'clock. She said Tim had left in a huff and had not returned.

"So you went to bed and just found out about your husband's death this morning when the police came to the door?" Dr. Quicksolve asked the petite young lady who sat at the kitchen table sobbing and wringing her hands.

"No," she said, getting up to pour Dr. Quicksolve a cup of coffee. Standing, she was barely over five feet tall and could just reach the coffee cups in the cupboard. Her hands trembled as she set the cup on the table in front of Dr. Quicksolve. "I was awake most of the night listening to music and worrying about Tim," she said.

"Had he left in a huff before?" Dr. Quicksolve asked.

"Yes," she said. "He doesn't talk things out. He just drives around and settles down. He's usually back in an hour or two. We both apologize, and the spat is forgotten."

"Did you hear the car drive in?" Lieutenant Rootumout asked.

"No, the music," she said.

"I'm afraid, Mrs. Contrary..." Lieutenant Rootumout began.

"That someone killed your husband, drove his car home, and left it here with his body in the back seat," Dr. Quicksolve said, finishing Lieutenant Rootumout's sentence.

Why didn't Dr. Quicksolve suspect Mary?

Solution on page 91.

Cattle Rustlers

• • • • • • • • •

Dr. J.L. Quicksolve and Junior sat in their VW Beetle just off the highway at the entrance to a cornfield. They were not exactly inconspicuous in the bright yellow car, but Dr. Quicksolve did not think that was important for this job. They certainly did not look like a police stakeout as they sat eating chili dogs and sipping root beer.

There had been a series of thefts in the area. It was actually cattle rustling. Cows had been stolen from farms while farmers had been working in distant fields. When Junior found out what his dad was going to do, he asked to come along. He put on a cowboy hat just for fun and to add a little atmosphere to the situation. Dr. Quicksolve had gone along with his son's sense of humor and donned a Stetson himself. So there they sat—a couple of real wranglers, cowboy hats and all—sitting in a yellow Bug in a cornfield, munching chili dogs.

As Dr. Quicksolve took his last bite, he got a call over the radio. A farmer named McDonald had just called. After returning from the fields, McDonald found five cows missing from his barn. He had seen a white truck just before he reached his house. He thought it might have been the rustlers.

Just then two white trucks passed Dr. Quicksolve and Junior. Both trucks were going west. One had a sign on the door that said "Solomon Produce—Canton, Ohio." The other truck's sign read "Spartan Trucking—Sheboygan, Michigan." The trucks reached a fork in the road. The Solomon truck traveled to the left, the Spartan truck to the right.

"Well," Dr. Quicksolve said to his son. "It must be one of those two trucks. Which one shall we follow?"

"I think you know as well as I do, Dad," Junior replied.

Which truck did Junior think belonged to the crooks?

Solution on page 86.

One Foggy Night

• • • • • • • • •

"City Bank was robbed, and a bulletin went out," Sergeant Rebekah Shurshot explained to Dr. J.L. Quicksolve. "Rookie Officer Goodheart was in the area. He reported picking up a man walking away in dense fog just outside town. Officer Goodheart said he arrested the man with the money bag from the robbery. He put the suspect in the back of his police car. The officer said he reached for the switch to turn on his bright lights while turning around and took his eyes off the road for just a second. He crashed in a ditch, and the suspect got away. Fortunately, he was in such a hurry he forgot the money bag. Officer Kautchya found a man running along the road in the fog and brought him in. Goodheart has not identified him yet. We're waiting for Officer Goodheart to get back from the hospital. It looks like he broke his arm in the crash. They're putting a cast on his arm now."

"What does the suspect say about all this?" Dr. Quicksolve said.

"The suspect, Ronnie Nose, said he was out jogging and got lost in the fog," Sergeant Shurshot replied. He lives nearby. I guess that's why he didn't need a car to rob the bank. He could walk home, and no one would suspect him in his own neighborhood—if they could see him at all in the fog. You can question him now."

"You talked to Officer Goodheart at the hospital?" Dr. Quicksolve asked.

"Yes. I came back here when I heard about the suspect," Sergeant Shurshot said.

"I am afraid we need to question our Rookie Officer Goodheart," Dr. Quicksolve said.

Why did Dr. Quicksolve want to question Officer Goodheart?

Solution on page 92.

Hijack

• • • • • • • •

"There have been hijackings of weapons shipments coming into the city," Captain Reelumin told Dr. J.L. Quicksolve. "The thieves have used disguises, false papers, and other tricks to steal weapons that have been sent into our country from the former Soviet Union. We don't know how they know when a shipment comes in or where they take it when they get it away from us. We are setting up a stakeout team near the harbor to watch what happens to a decoy shipment of weapons coming in tonight. Almost no one involved here knows it's not a real shipment of weapons. We hope the hijackers get it. Then we can follow them and get back what has already been taken. We're afraid we're dealing with clever terrorists."

Dr. Quicksolve and Captain Reelumin stood on a rooftop overlooking a warehouse. "The navy's scheduled to pick up our load of weapons from this warehouse. We'll see what happens," Captain Reelumin told Dr. Quicksolve. "Sergeant Shurshot is at the gate posing as a warehouse guard. She'll signal us if anything looks suspicious."

A large white truck pulled up to the gate. The sign on the side said "Norfolk Navel Base."

"Sergeant Shurshot is wearing a radio so we can hear her," Captain Reelumin said as the two men watched the uniformed driver hand papers to Sergeant Shurshot.

The sergeant looked at the papers she had been given. "Here to pick up some weapons, eh?" Sergeant Shurshot hesitated and put one hand over her mouth and scratched her head with the other hand.

"What is it?" Captain Reelumin spoke into his headset. "Is there a problem, Sergeant?"

"Any problem?" they heard the driver ask Sergeant Shurshot with what was clearly a southern accent.

"No," she said, composing herself. "No problem. I see your credentials match the sign on your truck. Very official. No problem."

"I guess she's figured out that's our crook," Dr. Quicksolve said. "Let's follow that truck."

What was Sergeant Shurshot's signal?

Solution on page 88.

Miss Cherry Blossom

· · · · · · · · ·

Dr. J.L. Quicksolve and Junior walked around the farm wagon, which was being transformed by a group of excited young people happily chatting as they worked on the Miss Cherry Blossom float the night before the Independence Day parade. Miss Cherry Blossom herself, Mary Schino, was introduced to Dr. Quicksolve. She asked the famous detective for his autograph for her younger brother and was flattered when he said, "Yes, of course, if I may have yours."

Dr. Quicksolve was up and out bright and early the next morning. He was concerned about the information Lieutenant Rootumout had received from an informer that a local gang of thugs was planning to rob a bank during the parade. The informer could not say which bank, though. Dr. Quicksolve was scheduled to be in the parade with Junior, who would be wearing a dog costume and asking people to "take a bite out of crime." The detective knew he would rather be dealing with the potential bank robbery.

As Dr. Quicksolve walked down the row of parking spaces reserved for parade entrants, he noticed a sign saying, "reserved for Miss Cherry Blossom." The float had not arrived yet, but there was a shiny convertible parked in the spot on the street in front of the Community Bank.

Sergeant Rebekah Shurshot stood in front of the convertible as Dr. Quicksolve approached. "Something about this car doesn't seem right," she told him.

Dr. Quicksolve walked around the car and said, "Call Lieutenant Rootumout. I think we may have found the bank and the getaway car."

Why did Dr. Quicksolve suspect this was the bank that would be robbed?

Solution on page 87.

Woof! Woof! Bang! Bang!

• • • • • • • •

The body of Shirley Stonedead lay face down on the stairs. One arm stretched up to the stair above her head. It almost looked as if she had fallen asleep on the stairs, except for the three bullet holes in her back. At the bottom of the steps lay a pit bull terrier. It had taken two bullets to stop the dog.

The police photographer was taking pictures as a tall man in a flashy suit, Barrie Scarrie, talked to Dr. J.L. Quicksolve and Sergeant Rebekah Shurshot. The long scar on the man's face seemed to make a smile impossible. "I had an early appointment with Miss Stonedead. She owed me money. I came to pick it up," Barrie said. "As I was just about to push the doorbell, I heard a dog bark and two shots. Then I heard a noise in the back of the house, and a car came backing out of the driveway and took off. I didn't see the driver, and I didn't recognize the car. The door of the house was unlocked, so I went in. I saw Miss Stonedead and her dead dog. I called the police. That's all I know."

"Have you known Miss Stonedead long?" Dr. Quicksolve asked.

"Yes, I have. I used to work here. I was her bodyguard," Barrie explained.

Dr. Quicksolve and Sergeant Shurshot stepped aside to listen to what Officer Longarm had found out. "The back door was broken open. A safe upstairs was jimmied open too. It's empty," Officer Longarm said. "It had to be a burglar. Did Mr. Scarrie give you a description of the suspect?" Officer Longarm asked Sergeant Shurshot.

"No," Sergeant Shurshot answered, "but I imagine he has a picture of the murderer in his wallet." Dr. Quicksolve chuckled at her little joke.

What did Sergeant Shurshot mean?

Solution on page 94.

Speedy Getaway

● ● ● ● ● ● ● ●

Dr. J.L. Quicksolve was driving west on Eisenhower Boulevard, heading out of town. He got a call on his cellular phone. It was Officer Longarm reporting a bank robbery. Dr. Quicksolve pulled his yellow VW Beetle to the side of the road while he listened to Officer Longarm.

The bank had been robbed by one gunman. Witnesses said the robber wore a shaggy beard and a baseball cap, and he had long hair tied in a ponytail. He said nothing. He handed the clerk a note demanding money and lifted his left hand just enough to show the gun. He ran out the door with a large bag of money and jumped into a waiting getaway car.

Dr. Quicksolve asked for a description of the car. "It was unique," Officer Longarm said. "It was a white Jaguar convertible. They had the top down, and the robber jumped in over the door. Witnesses said there

was a large dent in the driver's door. Otherwise, it looked as good as new. No one got a license number."

"That's an unusual getaway car," Dr. Quicksolve said. "Criminals usually don't want to be so conspicuous. They want to blend in and not get noticed."

"The getaway car headed west, but it could have turned anywhere," Officer Longarm said.

Dr. Quicksolve looked down the road ahead and saw two women waiting on the side of the road at a bus stop. One woman was sitting on a suitcase as they waited for a bus. Dr. Quicksolve slowly drove up to the bus stop and rolled down the passenger window of his car to talk to the women.

"Did you see any unusual cars drive by here recently?" he asked. "Any convertibles?"

"Yes, we did," one of the women said. "We saw a white Jaguar driving like crazy—headed west. The top was down, and it had a dent in the driver's door. It must be long gone by now."

Dr. Quicksolve thanked the women, pulled up half a block, and spoke into his phone. "Officer Longarm, I have two suspects."

Why did Dr. Quicksolve suspect the two women?

Solution on page 89.

B.B. Bigstuff

· · · · · · · · ·

"We arrested Bobby Bluntnose, the private detective, for murdering B.B. Bigstuff, the men's clothing tycoon. Then we had to let him go," Lieutenant Rootumout told Dr. J.L. Quicksolve as they sat in Dr. Quicksolve's library sipping coffee. "He had the motive. He had worked for B.B. Bigstuff as a security guard and was recently fired for making fun of short people. Remember, B.B. Bigstuff was only five-foot-one, but he sold clothing for extra-large men. He insisted on wearing large sizes, so his pants drooped and the sleeves of his suit jackets hung over his knuckles. He was quite a sight. Bobby Bluntnose also had the opportunity. He admits he was in Bigstuff's office, firing his revolver at the time of the murder."

Dr. Quicksolve scratched the head of his retriever, Copper, as if to help the dog think. Then he said, "Give me some more details."

"Bluntnose was in B.B.'s office at eight-forty-five according to B.B.'s secretary. On the way out he told the secretary B.B. was on the phone and should not be disturbed. He also said he would be back soon.

"Bluntnose came back a few minutes later. He was in the office just a couple minutes when the secretary heard two shots. A few seconds later Bluntnose ran out of the office with a gun in his hand and told the secretary to call the police. His story was that a woman shot Bigstuff through the window, and he shot at the assailant as she ran off. Bigstuff was killed with a .22 caliber bullet, and Bluntnose had a .38 with one shot fired. So it looks as if he's telling the truth," Lieutenant Rootumout said.

"There is a way he could have done it," Dr. Quicksolve said.

How?

Solution on page 94.

Disappearing Duffel

•••••••••

Junior had stayed after soccer practice to try a few extra shots on goal. He practiced dribbling at speed, angling across the goal to draw the keeper, and firing with either foot. There was no one else in the locker room when he finally came in.

Junior thought he heard the locker room door when he turned off the shower. He dried himself as he walked to his locker, and he heard the door again. Then he noticed his gym bag was gone. He wrapped his towel around his waist and ran out of the boys' locker room into the hallway. John Bigdood and Bobby Socks were drinking from the water fountain that separated the boys' and girls' locker rooms. No one else was around. Junior watched the two boys walk to the end of the hall and out the door.

The next morning Junior walked to school with Prissy Powers, the cutest girl on the cheerleading squad. He told her about his disappearing duffel bag. She suggested he ask the principal's secretary, Miss Notepad, if anyone had turned one in to the lost-and-found. They walked into the office as John Bigdood and Bobby Socks walked out. John was carrying his large football bag. Neither of them carried books.

Junior asked the secretary if anyone had turned in an athletic bag. She said, "Yes, one. It was John Bigdood's. It had his name on it. He just picked it up. Someone found it in the girls' locker room this morning. No other bags were turned in yet today."

"Well," Prissy said, "maybe somebody will turn yours in later today."

"I don't think it's going to be turned in. But if you get the principal, Miss Notepad," he said to the secretary, "I think we can get my bag back."

What does Junior suspect?

Solution on page 93.

Izzy Dizzy?

• • • • • • • • •

Dr. J.L. Quicksolve stood beside Sergeant
Rebekah Shurshot and watched the television
screen intently as Lieutenant Rootumout pushed
the buttons on the remote control. Horizontal
lines waved down and then up on the screen as
the fuzzy picture came into focus and revealed a
man back away from a bank teller's window and
walk out of the bank backwards. Lieutenant

Rootumout pushed the remote again. "Watch him as he comes into the bank. You get a pretty good look at his face," Lieutenant Rootumout said. They watched the robbery unfold. The man came in, looked boldly at the camera, and went ahead and robbed the bank under its watchful eye. Lieutenant Rootumout turned off the television as the robber disappeared out the bank door with a large sack of money.

"We have arrested a suspect, Izzy Clownen," Lieutenant Rootumout said.

"You have a clear picture. What's the problem?" Sergeant Shurshot said.

"Well, he looks just like the robber, but he has an alibi. Several people said he was at a bar across town. It looks like he has a foolproof alibi. They said he sat there for nearly two hours drinking. They said he was loud and drunk, calling attention to himself. One guy said he was dizzy. I guess he drank quite a lot. Finally, he just stood up and walked out the door. It looks like he's in two places at once."

"Is he?" Dr. Quicksolve asked "Or is he Dizzy?"

What did Dr. Quicksolve mean?

Solution on page 90.

Lady Hope

● ● ● ● ● ● ● ● ●

"I was just walking the puppy in the park right before lunch. We had stopped at a bush when somebody hit me from behind. He knocked me down, grabbed the puppy, dropped the note, and ran. I didn't get much of a look at him," Stuart Bones explained. He had been hired to walk his neighbor's dog.

Mr. Kaynine's new puppy had been dognapped. He explained, "I got this puppy from a friend of mine who's been raising world champion poodles. I had another friend who raised Newfoundlands. We were cross-breeding to get a dog that could swim well and look cute at the same time to be trained to do synchronized swimming. This puppy was my best hope. Because of my high hopes, I decided just this morning to name the puppy Lady Hope. I figured she would be a champion and get me going in the business. That's why she's so valuable to me."

"Read the note that was dropped beside Stuart when the dog was stolen," said Dr. Quicksolve, who had been asked to assist in the dognapping investigation, to Mr. Kaynine.

"It says, 'If you want to see your dog again, leave $10,000 at the park bench at the west end of the park tonight at midnight. Try any tricks and you'll never see Lady again!'

"I don't know what to do. That dog is very important to me," Mr. Kaynine said in desperation.

"Apparently Stu Bones knows just how important she is to you," Dr. Quicksolve said. He turned to Mr. Bones and said, "I think you had better show us where the dog has been taken."

Why did Dr. Quicksolve suspect Stu Bones?

Solution on page 88.

The Butler Didn't Do It

• • • • • • • • •

"The butler's body was found right here at the front door," Sergeant Rebekah Shurshot explained to Dr. J.L. Quicksolve as she pointed to the outline of a body drawn on the hardwood floor. Outlines like that always made Dr. Quicksolve think of the puzzles he used to put together as a boy. The missing piece now, though, was a dead body, and this was no game.

"Was anyone else in the house at the time?" asked Dr. Quicksolve.

"Yes, the maid was upstairs cleaning. She said she heard a single shot. She ran downstairs just in time to see two men run to a van and pull away. She couldn't give us much of a description of the two men," Sergeant Shurshot said.

Dr. Quicksolve looked around the house. It was in shambles. Drawers were pulled out, tables were overturned, and pictures were pulled off the walls. "Apparently they took a lot of things—valuable paintings, silverware, a large coin collection, televisions, stereo, etc. We haven't counted everything yet," the sergeant said.

"What about the owners of the house? Where are they?" Dr. Quicksolve asked.

"They're on vacation all this week. We're trying to locate them now. They don't even know about the robbery yet."

"I see. They just happened to be on vacation. When you get in touch with them, tell them they are going to need a new maid, as well as a new butler," Dr. Quicksolve said.

Why will they need a new maid?

Solution on page 92.

Stinker Jones

• • • • • • • • •

"Robert Jones was cynical, witty, and rich," lawyer Gladis Notmie told Dr. J.L. Quicksolve as they stood on the sidelines watching Junior's team play soccer. Gladis had called Dr. Quicksolve, wanting to talk to him. He said he planned to watch his son play soccer and she was welcome to come along. "He named his three children Ima. His two sons are Ima Stinker Jones and Ima Slick Jones. His daughter is Ima Prima Donna Jones. He called them by their middle names. Robert died and left a will that said everything he owned went to Ima Stinker, since Slick and Prima Donna each had successful businesses of their own. The problem, though, was that the fortune in stocks and bonds was placed in a large safe. No one knew the combination to the safe, and the will said Stinker had to find it on his own within one month or forfeit the fortune to his brother and sister."

"Did he find the combination to the safe?" Dr. Quicksolve asked.

"Well, according to him, yes and no. He said his father was very religious and constantly urged his children to read the Bible. Stinker figured that was a clue and his father may have left the combination in his Bible. He found his father's old Bible. He said there was a message written by his father on the first page. It said, 'Congratulations.

Read this verse and turn to page 1204.' That page had a note saying, 'Read this verse and turn to page 1243.' It went on directing him to read certain underlined verses and go on to another designated page."

"And where did it end?" Dr. Quicksolve asked.

"It didn't. Stinker said the last message directed him to page 1422. He said he found page 1421 and the next page was torn out! He claimed his brother and sister tore the page out so they could get his inheritance."

"I don't think they did," Dr. Quicksolve said.

Why didn't Dr. Quicksolve believe Stinker's story?

Solution on page 86.

Classroom Crime

• • • • • • • • •

Junior sat in Principal Paddlebottom's office. Junior's friend, Shortstop, sat next to him. Bobby Socks sat across the room from them. Mrs. Spellbinder, Junior's teacher, stood talking to Mr. Paddlebottom. She told the principal that she came in to school this morning, unlocked her room, put her purse in her classroom closet, and went to the teachers' workroom. She noticed Bobby Socks was painting the wall in the hall outside her room, but she did not think she needed to lock the door. When she got back, her closet door was open, and money was gone from her purse.

"Bobby was painting over some things that should not have been written on the wall in the first place," Mr. Paddlebottom said. Then he turned to Junior and Shortstop. "You two came in early today?"

"Yes," Junior said. "We saw Mrs. Spellbinder walking toward the teachers' workroom."

"And what else?" Mr. Paddlebottom asked.

Shortstop gulped nervously and said, "We saw Bobby Socks go into Mrs. Spellbinder's classroom. He came out a minute later and started painting again."

"Did you go into Mrs. Spellbinder's room Bobby?" Mr. Paddlebottom asked, turning to look at him.

"I was in there just a minute, like Shortstop said," Bobby replied. "I washed a little paint off my hands. I wasn't in there long enough to do anything else. Why don't you search Shortstop? He might have gone into the room when my back was turned," Bobby said.

"No one else has been in your room yet?" Mr. Paddlebottom asked Mrs. Spellbinder.

"I locked it after I saw the money was missing just a few minutes ago. I don't think anyone else has come into the building yet," Mrs. Spellbinder said.

Junior spoke up. "I think we can tell easily if Bobby is telling the truth."

What did Junior mean?

Solution on page 91.

Dark Suspicion

●●●●●●●●

"Does that man have a gun in his hand?" Sergeant Rebekah Shurshot asked Dr. J.L. Quicksolve. She was looking ahead into the darkness lit by the headlights of Dr. Quicksolve's VW Beetle. They saw a man cross the street and get into a mini-van parked on the side of the road. They were in an area known for drug deals. This looked suspicious.

"Call for backup," Dr. Quicksolve said as he pulled to the side of the road, watching the van in his side mirror.

Sergeant Shurshot did not take her eyes off the van sitting in the darkness as she reached for the microphone below the dash and made the call.

Dr. Quicksolve placed the portable flashing red light on his roof as they stepped out of the VW. They approached the dark van from each side. Sergeant Shurshot had her hand on her holstered pistol. Dr. Quicksolve's hand was inside his jacket.

They reached the van and asked the two men inside to step out of the vehicle. The two men got out of the van and closed the doors. They raised their hands as they began their protest. "What is this?" one asked.

"We didn't do anything!" the other added.

"Where's the gun?" Sergeant Shurshot demanded.

"There's no gun!" the driver said.

"We saw someone get into the van with a gun," Dr. Quicksolve said.

"Yeah," the driver said. "Some guy tried to rob us. He came over with that gun and climbed into our van. But then you pulled over and stopped. He saw that red light and got scared. When you got out of the car, he slipped out the other sliding door of the van and ran off."

"Show me," Dr. Quicksolve said.

They walked around the van, and the man opened the sliding door. Dr. Quicksolve smiled at what happened. Sergeant Shurshot shook her head. They could hear the sirens of approaching police cars. "We'll search the van when the back-up arrives," she said.

What happened when the driver opened the sliding door that made Dr. Quicksolve grin?

Solution on page 92.

Train Robbery

• • • • • • • •

"We had three people on the train," said Carl Crossdraw, head of security for the Glistening Rocks Diamond Corporation. "Paula Perchlip, our courier, had the satchel of diamonds handcuffed to her wrist. We had two armed guards in the passenger car with her. She got up to use the rest room. She started to go to another train car because the rest room in hers was out of order. When she left the car, a man grabbed her. She said she fought with him for several minutes before she lost her balance and fell off the train. Two women were waiting. They jumped on her before she stopped rolling and took the satchel. Our two guards went to check on her when she didn't come back. They couldn't find her anywhere on the train, so they called us. We called the police."

Dr. J.L. Quicksolve and Captain Reelumin listened intently as Mr. Crossdraw finished his story about how nearly a million dollars worth of uncut diamonds were stolen from a train.

"Paula was found along the tracks later by state troopers," Crossdraw said. "She was bruised up a bit. She still had half of the handcuffs on her wrist. She said the women who grabbed her cut the handcuffs off with bolt cutters, grabbed the satchel, and ran off. She didn't see a getaway car or anything. Fortunately, the state police were really on the ball, and the two women were caught speeding down the highway.

"Paula, of course, is a hero for putting up such a fight. We would like to have you present an award to her for us, if you would," the security man said to Dr. Quicksolve.

"I wonder if a warrant for her arrest might be more appropriate than an award," Dr. Quicksolve said.

Why did he suspect Paula was in on the robbery?

Solution on page 86.

Ben Comes Back

· · · · · · · ·

Dr. J.L. Quicksolve did not care much for Benjamin Clayborn Blowhard, Sergeant Rebekah Shurshot's friend. His loud, bragging, haughty, know-it-all attitude and preposterous stories were quite counter to Dr. Quicksolve's personal modesty and devotion to the truth. Yet, for some reason, when Blowhard was not around for a while, Dr. Quicksolve found himself making excuses for him in his own mind. His stories certainly entertained people, even Junior who saw right through them. Sometimes Dr. Quicksolve almost thought of Benjamin Clayborn Blowhard as a friend or at least a tolerable acquaintance. So when Dr. Quicksolve heard Blowhard was coming to town again, he had mixed feelings at first. He resigned himself to it and even began to look forward to the stories.

Then Blowhard's crazy stories got him into big trouble. Somebody actually believed them and decided Benjamin Clayborn Blowhard was a man worth kidnapping.

A Hidden Message

• • • • • • • • •

"Dr. Quicksolve?" the man on the line asked Dr. J.L. Quicksolve. "Drake D. Peeper, C.I.A., here," he said without waiting for an answer.

"Yes. How are you, Drake?" Dr. Quicksolve said into the telephone.

"Good. Good." The agent said. "A strange thing here."

"What is it?" Dr. Quicksolve asked.

"We got this letter. It's a message cut out from various magazines and such. I think you'd better take a look."

"Okay, Drake. I'll be right over."

When Dr. Quicksolve arrived at Peeper's office the letter was spread out on a table. It was written from letters cut from various sources, as Peeper had said. It said, "We have your Agent Blowhard. Have two million dollars ready when we call or he dies."

"We don't have an Agent Blowhard, so we thought it was a prank," Peeper explained.

"Then we got the call. We told them to forget it. We also traced the call. We found where they called from, a motel outside of town. There we found prints of a known terrorist who goes by the name of Simon Smudge. We heard this Benjamin Clayborn Blowhard was a friend of yours."

"Something like that," Dr. Quicksolve said. "Did you find anything else?"

"Only some scraps of paper where they cut the letters out, and in another room we found this newspaper."

Dr. Quicksolve took the newspaper and opened it. One article had several letters underlined, as if someone was playing a game—"<u>A</u> <u>n</u>ews <u>bu</u>lletin <u>c</u>ame in to<u>d</u>ay saying papers ta<u>ke</u>n from the Whit<u>e</u> House contained fingerprints..."

"The problem, of course, is we do not know where to look next," Peeper said.

"I think we do," Dr. Quicksolve said.

What has Dr. Quicksolve figured out?

Solution on page 88.

Hideout

• • • • • • • •

Dr. J.L. Quicksolve got descriptions of the international terrorist Simon Smudge and two known accomplices. Those descriptions fitted three men who had rented a room at the Driftwood Motel, where evidence of the kidnapping was found. The same descriptions fitted three men who had rented a secluded cottage on North Lake.

Agent Drake D. Peeper and three other men from the C.I.A. were crammed into Dr. Quicksolve's yellow VW as they drove down the narrow dirt road to the cottage. The fog was so thick Dr.

Quicksolve was forced to drive very slowly through the darkness.

They stopped and parked the car at what they figured was about 50 yards from the cottage. Agent Peeper told one of his men to stay with the car. Everyone else fanned out in the darkness and approached the cottage. As they got closer they saw that lights were on, and they heard loud music.

"You don't play loud music in a hideout," Dr. Quicksolve said to Agent Peeper. "They know we're out here!"

Suddenly they heard the roar of a motor beyond the cottage at the edge of the lake. They stumbled through the dense fog to the shore of the lake seconds after a small motorboat pulled away from the dock. One of the agents jumped into a second boat and started it immediately.

"The car!" Dr. Quicksolve shouted to Agent Peeper. They both turned and ran back toward the road.

Why did Dr. Quicksolve suddenly think of the car?

Solution on page 93.

Brazilian Story

•••••••••

Dr. J.L. Quicksolve and Sergeant Rebekah Shurshot sat with Junior drinking coffee and listening to Benjamin Clayborn Blowhard brag about how he had escaped from the terrorists who had kidnapped him. Junior, who was eating his favorite ice cream treat, a freight train, noticed Ben did not mention that he was found sitting, tied up and gagged, in a motorboat speeding across a lake, headed for certain disaster. Nor did he mention anyone else's part in his rescue.

It began when Dr. Quicksolve congratulated

Blowhard for leaving the message Dr. Quicksolve had figured out to learn where the terrorists were taking their prisoner. Blowhard took it from there, talking about his confidence in the clue he had left behind and how courageous he was throughout the ordeal.

"It's my background in government work," he continued. "I have done a lot of work with languages, secret codes, and stuff. I worked with the Brazilian Army Intelligence last year. I had to interpret a message from Portugal. They were pretty good. They figured out the code quickly after I did the translation. Then the C.I.A. had to fly me out in a hurry. There was an emergency. They needed my help again."

"But Agent Peeper said you were not with the C.I.A.," Junior said.

"'Affiliated' is the word," Blowhard said. "Of course, they won't admit it. It's hush-hush."

"So you helped the Brazilian Army Intelligence?" Junior asked.

"That's right," Blowhard answered. "But enough about me."

Dr. Quicksolve agreed, and refrained from asking the obvious question about Benjamin Clayborn Blowhard's story.

What was the obvious question?

Solution on page 87.

Blowing in the Wind

• • • • • • • • •

"So what was the big emergency you had to fly off to deal with?" Junior asked Benjamin Clayborn Blowhard as Dr. J.L. Quicksolve, Sergeant Rebekah Shurshot, and Ben Blowhard continued sipping their coffee. Junior was finishing the second half of his freight train ice cream treat, which came in two glass bowls shaped like a train.

"I can't tell you where the C.I.A. took me, but I was needed to fly a glider plane to make a quiet delivery, if you know what I mean. I had to cover quite a distance, about 70 miles. It was an old glider, and they had trouble starting the engine to get me off the ground. Once in the air, I turned off the engine and glided quietly through the sky. That is quite an experience.

"I watched for clouds and birds that were rising without flapping their wings so I could use the updraft to go higher. I spotted a small city and pointed the plane up to glide as high as I could so they would not spot me and interrupt my mission. I kept the nose up and rose higher and higher for quite some time, until I was sure I would be just a speck in the sky to anyone down there on the ground. I flew silently, like a bird."

"Did you make your delivery?" Sergeant Shurshot asked.

"Sure," Blowhard said. "No problems."

Junior, setting aside the two empty freight train bowls to take home and add to his collection, looked up with a questioning glance at his father. Dr. Quicksolve had an equally puzzled look on his face. As usual, something was wrong with Benjamin Clayborn Blowhard's tale of adventure. Dr. Quicksolve winked at Junior, and neither of them said anything as Ben went on with yet another incredible yarn.

What did Dr. Quicksolve and Junior notice? Why were they so puzzled?

Solution on page 91.

The Thief's Glove

•••••••••

"There were three people here at the service station when the money was stolen," Officer Longarm told Dr. J.L. Quicksolve as they stood in front of the gas station. "Rod Ratchet, the mechanic, said he was out back putting stuff in the dumpster. Terry Tidiup, who cleans up the place, said he was mopping the rest room. Bubba Bobbob, the cashier, was closing up. Bobbob said he was in the office counting the money on the desk when he remembered he had forgotten to lock the front door to close up for the night. He got up to lock it, leaving the money on the desk. When he was walking back toward the office, he saw a gloved hand reach from the door to the garage and grab a handful of bills."

A tall, thin man with short hair and a long chin came out the station door. "This is Bubba Bobbob," Officer Longarm told Dr. Quicksolve.

"You saw someone take the money?" Dr. Quicksolve asked Bubba.

"Well, I saw a hand—a glove, really. It was a dirty, tan work glove. I didn't see who was wearing it. It looked like gloves Rod wears sometimes. I can't say it was him, though. I can't believe it was him."

"Did you tell Rod and Terry what you saw?" Dr. Quicksolve asked.

"Only what I told you," Bubba answered. "I saw a gloved hand."

"Let's go talk to Rod," the detective said, turning to enter the open garage door.

A second man came around the corner of the building. He was short and heavy. "I found the other glove," he said, waving it in the air.

"Where did you find it, Terry?" Officer Longarm asked the cleaning man.

"It was behind the dumpster, out back," Terry answered. "It's one of Rod's," he added.

"Let's talk to Rod," Officer Longarm said.

"Good idea," said Dr. Quicksolve. "Then you can probably arrest Terry."

Why did Dr. Quicksolve suspect Terry?

Solution on page 92.

The Late Cal Culator

• • • • • • • •

Dr. J.L. Quicksolve liked late night talk shows because of the comedy. Humor usually involves looking at things in different ways, and Dr. Quicksolve found it an excellent exercise for a detective. It also helped him relax. The ring of the phone interrupted his TV watching. Some interruptions can be pleasant, but not murder.

Sergeant Rebekah Shurshot pulled up to the house in her police car just as Dr. Quicksolve arrived in his yellow VW Beetle. A young man was standing in front of the house in his pajamas and robe. His feet were bare. "I'm Don Dunital. I'm a student at the university, and I live here with my roommate, Cal Culator. Or should I say 'lived'? He's dead. He's in the house on the floor."

Dr. Quicksolve and Sergeant Shurshot walked into the house. Sergeant Shurshot flipped on the light switch and gasped at the amount of blood on the floor around the body. She collected herself quickly and checked the body for signs of life. "Dead," she said.

Don Dunital came into the house behind them. "I came downstairs to get a midnight snack when I found Cal's body lying here. I was so scared and upset I just ran out the door. I went to the neighbor's and called the police. Then I waited out in front for somebody to get here. I haven't searched the house or anything. I suppose the killer could still be in here somewhere," Don said.

"You could be right about that," Sergeant Shurshot said.

"I am pretty sure you are right," Dr. Quicksolve said.

What did Dr. Quicksolve mean?

Solution on page 93.

Pretty Rings in a Row

• • • • • • • • •

Dr. Quicksolve and Junior were at the edge of town when the call came over the radio. Lucy Looker's diamond ring collection was missing. No one could figure out what happened. They needed Dr. Quicksolve.

Junior was amazed at the size of Lucy Looker's colossal mansion as they drove up the long circular drive and stopped in front of the huge white pillars that marked the entrance to the palacelike home. But Junior was not quite as amazed at what he saw as was the servant who watched the yellow VW Beetle with a canoe lashed to its roof pull up in front of the mansion and dispense a tall man and a boy dressed for camping and fishing.

Lucy Looker, the actress, told Dr. Quicksolve about the missing diamond rings as they walked to the back of the house. "I don't insist or anything," she said, "but every man I have married so far has given me a ring with a bigger diamond than the last one. I had a very valuable collection of six diamond rings. I like to put them in a row according to size. Now they're gone. They disappeared right off my dresser this morning."

Dr. Quicksolve, Junior, Lieutenant Rootumout, and Lucy Looker sat on the back patio of her mansion, sipping cool drinks and watching a handsome man of about 30 whacking tennis balls over a net as a machine shot them across to him.

"I'll get it!" Junior said when one of the balls sailed high over the eight-foot fence at the other end of the court.

"No!" the man shouted. "I collect them up when I'm done!"

A teenage girl swam laps in the pool. She rolled onto her back in the water and waved at Junior before swimming a length of backstroke.

"Who was here?" Dr. Quicksolve asked.

"My servants—I've had them for years," Lucy answered. "My niece, Hannah," she indicated the girl in the pool, "and my current man-friend, Jean-Luc," she said, raising her glass toward the tennis player.

"We have searched the house as thoroughly as possible. I believe they're gone," Lieutenant Rootumout said. "I don't see how, though, since no one has left," he added.

"If they aren't here, there is one most likely place they could be," Dr. Quicksolve said.

Where did Dr. Quicksolve think the diamond rings might be?

Solution on page 93.

The One-Armed Man

• • • • • • • • •

Lucy Looker, the actress, was very grateful to Dr. J.L. Quicksolve for solving her case and getting her missing diamonds back. She insisted he let her take him out to dinner at a fancy restaurant. She picked him up in her sporty convertible. Dr. Quicksolve was surprised at her knowledge of cars. She was fascinated by his story of how he had souped up the Porsche engine in his VW Beetle and strengthened the structure around the passenger area. "I even had air bags installed," Dr. Quicksolve was saying when Lucy's cellular phone rang.

"It's for you," she said, handing Dr. Quicksolve the small phone.

Dr. Quicksolve talked on the phone briefly. Then he asked Lucy, "Would you mind a small deviation in our plans? There's been a bank robbery. It shouldn't take long."

"The teller insists the bank robber was a one-armed man," Sergeant Rebekah Shurshot told Dr. Quicksolve when he and Lucy had arrived at the bank.

Overhearing this, a small man with round glasses jumped up and said, "It was a one-armed man!"

"Please calm down, Mr. Spectacle," Sergeant Shurshot said.

Mr. Spectacle sat down, and Sergeant Shurshot turned back to Dr. Quicksolve. "The robber wore a mask," she said. "We do have two suspects, though. They're filling out forms over there." Sergeant Shurshot nodded her head to indicate two men across the room who were seated next to each other, writing. "We had several police cars in the area and got there quickly when the alarm was set off," Sergeant Shurshot continued. "It has to be one of the two."

Dr. Quicksolve looked at the two men. "Find out which arm was missing and you should have your robber," he said. "Now, I have a dinner reservation waiting."

Sergeant Shurshot looked at the two men and back at Dr. Quicksolve. She smiled and nodded her head. "Enjoy your dinner," she said.

What could Dr. Quicksolve have noticed that would have made the solution so easy?

Solution on page 86.

Copper's Courage

• • • • • • • • •

Copper loved to accompany Junior on his paper route. The rust-colored retriever usually led the way, serving a useful purpose by distracting other dogs that might be a problem for Junior. Some dogs love to chase boys and girls on bikes, and a few dogs get a little too excited and take a nip at a pant leg or an ankle. But Copper drew away the attention of other dogs. Copper always ran by, leading a merry chase while Junior delivered the paper—except once.

On that day Junior had gotten off his bike to deliver the paper. Copper was about two houses ahead, as usual. Suddenly a pair of large dogs raced from a house behind Junior. The two dogs came roaring down the street toward Copper, barking with enthusiasm like hounds on a chase. Junior turned toward them as they approached. He held up his hands and shouted, "No! No!"

Just as the two charging animals were about to split and pass Junior on either side, Copper shot by Junior and hit both dogs like a charging bull. All three dogs rolled in a snarling ball of fur. One dog was catapulted away and lay whimpering on the grass. Copper held the other attacker down, growling and threatening, his teeth held close to the other dog's throat.

"Stop him! Stop him!" shouted a woman who came running from a house down the block.

"Copper," Junior said. Copper backed off the dog who rolled over and slowly got to his feet.

The woman checked her dogs for injuries and led them home.

Junior bent down, gave Copper a hug, and quietly said, "Good boy."

Why did Junior say, "Good boy"? Why did Copper attack instead of running away?

Solution on page 92.

Diversion

• • • • • • • •

Dr. J.L. Quicksolve sat on a park bench munching popcorn from a brown bag. Captain Reelumin sat next to him sipping a soft drink.

"We're planning to set up a net to trap a couple

of guys who've been robbing stores and banks out in Boondock Township," Captain Reelumin told Dr. Quicksolve. "You might like to come along."

"Tell me about it," Dr. Quicksolve said.

"It looks as if the thugs call for an ambulance to divert attention and then rob some place nearby. I talked to H.M. Moe, the Boondock Hospital administrator, and his two ambulance drivers. They're going to let us know when they get a call, and we'll surround the area with police cars. Up until now, the robbers seem to disappear into thin air. About 20 minutes after the ambulance call reporting some fake emergency, a small isolated bank or store gets robbed by two men wearing masks and coveralls. They always tie up and blindfold their victims to give themselves plenty of time to get away. The local police have been on alert, but they haven't seen anyone speeding away or any unusual traffic. No one has seen any strangers in the area. It seems to be someone local or someone able to disappear into thin air, as I said. Right now we don't have any suspects at all."

"You do have suspects," Dr. Quicksolve said, "and I have a suggestion about your trap."

Whom did Dr. Quicksolve suspect?

Solution on page 90.

Boomer Bash

• • • • • • • • •

The Boomer Bash was a gathering of hundreds (now dwindled down from the original thousands) of Flower Children from the Sixties (now middle-aged) who met in the Colorado mountains each year to remember their younger days of long hair, flower necklaces, bell-bottom pants, and noisy rebellion. Everything was the same, except bell-bottoms were hard to get and the old ones didn't fit anymore. The scene was noisy, though harmless, and quite frightening to a modern teenager.

The main feature of the Boomer Bash was the Battle of the Bands. Dozens of would-be famous rock groups who had never made it big competed for dubious distinctions such as loudest, rowdiest, silliest, and most obnoxious. Musical talent was never discussed. Five-foot trophies were provided for the winners of each category. It was only the chance to compete in this battle that brought together a strange group of men in a nearby hillside mansion. They called themselves Rat Cliff.

Rat Cliff and The Lemmings

● ● ● ● ● ● ● ● ●

The idea in the Sixties was to choose the strangest name you could think of for your band. If it upset people, all the better. That's how four young men—Abel, Birch, Cain, and Dirk—chose the name Rat Cliff. Their girlfriends, who had not yet caught on to the concept of liberation, provided backup noise and allowed themselves to be called "The Lemmings." Supporting the notion that women often mature early, The Lemmings broke away from Rat Cliff and became real people. When the band broke up, Dirk disappeared.

Falling into the trap of greed, Abel, Birch, and Cain became highly competitive and extremely wealthy through various business endeavors.

Each year they paused on their road to becoming grumpy old men to meet for a week at Abel's castlelike mansion in the mountains to practice for the Battle of the Bands competition. This year two new people had been invited. Cain brought along a strangely quiet guitar player, who called himself Iceman, to replace Dirk. Abel invited a famous detective by the name of Dr. J.L. Quicksolve.

Rat Cliff—One Down

• • • • • • • •

Dr. J.L. Quicksolve was the last to arrive and the first to see the body. A party was going on when Dr. Quicksolve arrived on his motorcycle. He had asked Abel's young wife, Evensong, for directions to the rest room. She sent him to her bedroom suite, saying she thought her husband had just finished showering. He was finished.

Dr. Quicksolve knocked and slowly opened the bathroom door. Abel's body lay in a puddle on the floor. A towel was wrapped around his waist. The shower curtain was pulled down and covered half his body, as if he had clutched it as he fell. A hair dryer lay in the water. Dr. Quicksolve reached his foot across the puddle and pushed at the plug until it fell out of the socket on the wall.

Everyone was upset, but the party did not stop.

Evensong, a particularly strong woman, held herself together well. She insisted to Dr. Quicksolve that her husband could never be stupid enough to cause such an accident. She believed he had been murdered. She said he would want the party to continue. She talked everyone into staying and convinced Dr. Quicksolve that she needed his help to catch her husband's killer and to take his place as drummer in the band.

The problem, of course, was finding the murderer, if there was one. Dr. Quicksolve quickly learned the two original, remaining band members had motives. Cain had been a longtime business rival of Abel's and had suffered several financial defeats at Abel's hands over the past few years. Birch had been a rival in love when the Lemmings were with the band and had always blamed Abel and Cain for the women leaving. He remained bitter.

The problem now was alibis. Cain had gone into town with Abel's chauffeur to buy guitar strings. Birch had been having breakfast with Evensong the whole time Abel was in the shower.

Iceman asked the obvious, "How could this be murder?"

"Your name gives me an idea," Dr. Quicksolve answered.

What did Dr. Quicksolve suspect?

Solution on page 95.

Rat Cliff—
Birch at Breakfast

• • • • • • • •

Evensong believed someone in the band must have killed her husband. She tried to keep a happy face and encourage the partying and practicing to continue. She also encouraged the band members to stay together in the mansion so she and Dr. J.L. Quicksolve could watch them and learn who killed her husband. The fourth morning, however, one got away.

They had all sat down for breakfast in their usual places when Cain, who had hardly sipped his coffee, stood up. He said, "I am going to ask your chauffeur to drive me to town, if you don't mind. I'm not comfortable driving in these mountains." He was gone from the room before Evensong had time to say that indeed she did mind.

The maid continued serving breakfast. Everyone except Iceman seemed more than a little nervous, remembering how Cain had also been gone when Abel had been murdered. Dr. Quicksolve was wary.

He was the first to react, pushing himself away from the table and dropping to the floor as the window behind Birch exploded, filling the air with flying glass.

The stillness of the room was as shocking as the sudden shower of glass. Everyone had ducked or dived and now slowly uncovered their eyes to see what had happened. Birch lay slumped over his breakfast with an arrow in his back.

When the sheriff arrived, he and Dr. Quicksolve walked outside and found the bow that had released the arrow nailed to a tree stump. Strangely, on such a dry mountain morning, the stump was wet and water still dripped down its sides.

"Someone must have been out here to shoot this thing," the sheriff said.

"Not necessarily out here," Dr. Quicksolve said.

What did Dr. Quicksolve suspect this time?

Solution on page 91.

Rat Cliff—Cain Is Slain

• • • • • • • • •

When Dr. J.L. Quicksolve and the sheriff came back inside, Dr. Quicksolve suggested they talk to Cain and the Iceman. Evensong said they had left together in Cain's car.

The sheriff knew his mountain roads well and sped through the twisting turns while Dr. Quicksolve clung tightly to his seat. Suddenly Dr. Quicksolve yelled, "Stop!"

The car slid to a stop. The sheriff followed Dr. Quicksolve's eyes and looked back. He saw what Dr. Quicksolve had seen on the last curve. The brush had been bent down at the mountain's edge about the width of a car.

The two men walked to the spot where the brush was bent and looked down the steep mountainside to see Cain's car overturned and in flames. Dr. Quicksolve bent down and felt a muddy puddle at the very edge of the cliff where the tire marks disappeared into empty space.

"The Iceman," Dr. Quicksolve said.

They found the body of Cain in the car. He was killed from the crushing fall. The Iceman was not around.

"You had better put out a bulletin for the Iceman, sheriff," Dr. Quicksolve said. "Arrest him for the murders of Abel, Birch, and Cain."

"Why do you suspect him? And how did he kill Cain?" the sheriff asked.

"It's all in a name," Dr. Quicksolve answered. "Vanity," he said.

What was Dr. Quicksolve talking about?

Solution on page 94.

Fetching Alibis

● ● ● ● ● ● ● ●

Dr. J.L. Quicksolve turned off Main Street into a small city park on the river. Three police cars were parked as if they had all converged at once to surround a single park bench. Another police car had stopped a blue sedan on the other side of the narrow river. "It must be quiet at the dough-nut shop," Junior quipped.

They had gotten a call about an early morning break-in at the Collector's Coin and Stamp Shop, which was just up a steep, wooded slope a short distance across the park.

A man in a suede jacket and baseball cap sat on the bench holding the collar of a very wet golden retriever. The dog stood up and shook himself, forcing the police officers to step back to avoid getting a shower.

"Looks like our dog, Copper," Junior said.

Lieutenant Rootumout held a cellular phone to his ear. "Stamps," he said to Dr. Quicksolve. "An envelope of stamps worth several thousands of dollars was stolen. A suspect was seen running into the park. This guy here said he was walking his dog and didn't see anything. He said he was throwing sticks into the river for his dog to fetch."

"There's something wrong with this picture," Dr. Quicksolve said, looking at the man on the bench petting his wet dog.

"The man seen running from the shop didn't have a dog." Lieutenant Rootumout said.

"Have you searched the men and the car on the other side of the river?" Dr. Quicksolve asked Lieutenant Rootumout.

"They are just about to do that," the lieutenant said, looking across the river.

"Do they know what to look for?" Dr. Quicksolve asked.

What did Dr. Quicksolve think the policemen across the river should be looking for?

Solution on page 88.

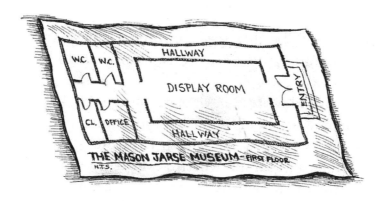

The Mason Jarse Museum

• • • • • • • • •

Mason Jarse was very proud of the large 19th century mansion he had converted into an art museum. "I have kept the outside of the building perfectly authentic, but, of course, the inside needed to be redesigned to best display the art," he told Dr. J.L. Quicksolve and his insurance friend, Fred Fraudstop. The museum owner was giving a personal tour as dozens of people walked around enjoying the art on display, sipping drinks and chatting about individual paintings and sculpture.

The interior had, indeed, been redesigned. Each of the two floors had a central display room. The display rooms were surrounded by walls that formed a rectangular hall around them. Two wide doorways were on opposite ends of the central rooms. There were two rest rooms, a custodial closet, and one small office. Except for the basement, there were no other rooms.

"The interior, of course, is not 19th century. It

is, after all, an art museum. I designed the interior to display the art the best way possible," Mr. Jarse continued. "We kept the high ceilings, as you can see, and put beautiful chandeliers at the center of each ceiling in the main display rooms."

"What about security?" Dr. Quicksolve asked.

"We have alarms set at the doors and windows," Mr. Jarse answered.

"I keep telling him that is not enough," Fred Fraudstop said. "He needs motion detectors too."

"I agree with Fred," Dr. Quicksolve said. "You have a fortune in paintings here."

"But those detectors with their plastic designs and little lights are so distracting," Mr. Jarse protested. "There is a silent alarm at all possible entries. If anyone broke in, the police would be here before they could get away."

"I wish I could convince you before it is too late," Fred Fraudstop said to Mason Jarse.

"Maybe together we can," Dr. Quicksolve said.

The museum closed at 11 o'clock that evening. Mason Jarse was called at midnight and told the alarm had been tripped at his museum. When he arrived, Dr. Quicksolve and Fred Fraudstop sat on the front porch of the museum. The door was open. "Don't worry," Fred told Mr. Jarse. "Nothing's been stolen. We just wanted to prove a point."

What had they done?

Solution on page 89.

Answers

• • • • • • • • •

Cattle Rustlers (page 22)—Junior knew there was a Canton in several states, including Ohio. Cheboygan, Michigan, though, unlike Sheboygan, Wisconsin, is spelled with a "C." They told the police to follow the Spartan truck.

Train Robbery (page 50)—Paula said she went to the rest room and then fought with a man for several minutes before falling off the train where two women immediately jumped on her and took the diamonds. How could the two women have known exactly where Paula was going to "fall" off the train unless they had planned the whole thing together?

The One-Armed Man (page 68)—Dr. Quicksolve saw that one man was right-handed and the other was left-handed. If one of them was the robber, he pretended to have only one arm by hiding the other inside his coat to fool the witnesses and police. Of course, he would keep out the arm he used best—left or right.

Stinker Jones (page 44)—Stinker said he found page 1421, but 1422 was missing. This could not be true, because books are numbered with odd numbers on the right and even numbers on the left. Page 1422 would be on the opposite side of page 1421. You could not tear out one without tearing out the other.

Country Killing (page 18)—Spinner Webb said he could see through the small crack in the door that the house had been ransacked, yet it was so dark he tripped over his aunt's body. If he could see it was ransacked through the crack, he should have seen the body with the light from the open door. He probably killed his aunt, locked the chain, went out the window, and then broke down the door to set the scene for his story.

Maps and Treats (page 8)—When they looked at the maps showing the directions their adventures had taken them each day, Flora and Fauna could see that Junior had written W-E-L-L. They ran to the well, cranked up the bucket, and found tickets to the rodeo that would be in town that Friday when Grandpa came home.

Miss Cherry Blossom (page 28)—Dr. Quicksolve thought a convertible in a parade entrant's parking space would make a good getaway car because no one would be suspicious. He knew, though, that Miss Cherry Blossom's float was a wagon. He checked the back of the convertible for the trailer hitch needed to pull the float. When he saw there was no hitch, he had reason to be very suspicious.

Brazilian Story (page 58)—Why did Benjamin Clayborn Blowhard have to translate a message from Portugal for the Brazilians when Portuguese is the official language of Brazil?

Hijack (page 26)—Sergeant Shurshot said the papers matched the sign on the truck. The word used for a navy base should be "naval," not "navel." A navel is a belly button.

Foul Play (page 6)—Dr. Quicksolve knew that Calvin Callumwright was a football referee. It seemed that as he lay dying he had put his hands in position to signal "holding," meaning Holden was the killer.

Fetching Alibis (page 82)—Of course, they should be looking for the stamps. The other thing they should look for is a dog's leash. Dr. Quicksolve noticed the man on the bench was holding the dog's collar and did not have a leash. He suspected the two men were working together. The man across the river brought the dog to send across the river to fetch the stolen stamps from the thief. This scheme gave both men an alibi. One was on the wrong side of the river, and the other one was playing with his dog.

A Hidden Message (page 54)—He can see Blowhard left them a clue. If you take the underlined letters—A-N-B-L-C-A-D-K-E-E and cross out the alphabetical letters (A,B,C,D,E), you are left with a message—N. LAKE, i.e., North Lake.

Lady Hope (page 40)—The dog had just received her name that morning, yet the ransom note, dropped before lunch, contained the dog's name.

A Ride with Grandma (page 14)—Apple trees are grafted. A branch from one tree is attached to a new tree. That's how you know what kind of apple you will get from a new tree. Since you can graft different kinds of apples to the same tree, you could not guess very well how many kinds of apples might come from four trees.

Also, Junior figured he could not guess because he already knew the answer.

Speedy Getaway (page 32)—It is unlikely that bank robbers would use such an unusual car unless they planned to get rid of it quickly. The two women could not have seen a dent on the driver's side of a car going the same direction as Dr. Quicksolve because they were at the bus stop on the right-hand side of the road where Dr. Quicksolve had to roll down the passenger window to talk with them. The bearded bank robber who did not speak could easily have been a woman in disguise. Dr. Quicksolve suspected the women ditched the car nearby and told the story about the passing Jaguar to steer the police away from them.

The Mason Jarse Museum (page 84)—Dr. Quicksolve and his friend simply stayed in the museum after it was closed. Had they been thieves, they could have taken their time getting whatever they wanted, placing everything near the door. They could then have exited quickly and would have been gone before the police arrived. Mr. Jarse was persuaded to install motion detectors.

Sick Trick (page 16)—He had four reasons.

1. He was suspicious about the missing ketchup and the thick "blood" on his cousin.

2. Junior knew Fauna rode correctly, on the right side of the road. She would have seen a car coming and probably avoided it.

3. A car was not likely to be speeding so recklessly in a school zone.

4. Amnesia victims lose their memories to some degree; they do not think they are dogs.

You probably thought of even more clues!

Diversion (page 72)—Dr. Quicksolve suspected that an accomplice made the emergency calls and then the ambulance drivers went out and robbed places on their way back from the phony emergencies. He noticed that the robberies happened about 20 minutes after the phony emergencies instead of while the police and ambulance were rushing to the scene. Coveralls would cover the ambulance drivers' uniforms, and tying and blindfolding the victims would prevent them from seeing the getaway car was an ambulance.

Izzy Dizzy? (page 38)—Dr. Quicksolve knew one man could not be in two places at once, as the evidence implied. But two men who looked alike could make it seem that way. Dr. Quicksolve suspected Izzy might have had a twin named Dizzy, because Lieutenant Rootumout had said, "One guy said he was dizzy." Dizzy may have acted up in the bar to provide an alibi for his twin, Izzy.

Rat Cliff—Birch at Breakfast (page 78)—Again the name Iceman was the clue. Dr. Quicksolve thought the bowstring might have been pulled back and somehow frozen on a block of ice. The ice would melt slowly, giving the murderer or murderers time to be somewhere else when the arrow was released.

Mary Contrary (page 20)—Dr. Quicksolve noticed the car seat had to be moved forward to remove the body. Someone had put the body in the back and then moved the seat back, wedging the body in between the seats. Being only five feet tall, Mary would have moved the seat forward. It was also doubtful, of course, that such a petite woman would have been able to lift the body of a full-grown man in the first place.

Blowing in the Wind (page 60)—Dr. Quicksolve and Junior noticed Benjamin Clayborn Blowhard obviously knew something about gliders. He said he looked for clouds that provide updrafts and birds flying up without flapping their wings, evidence of updrafts. Since gliders sometimes have small engines they use during takeoffs, that was no problem. But Blowhard said he "pointed the plane up" to rise. This is wrong. Gliders are kept pointed slightly downward, even as they use an updraft to rise.

Classroom Crime (page 46)—If Bobby was only in the room a minute and used that time to wash his hands, the sink would be wet. If he is lying, and he took time to steal the money, the sink would be dry.

The Butler Didn't Do It (page 42)—From the maid's story, it sounded as if the robbers rang the bell, shot, and ran. That would not have given them time to ransack the house the way they did. Her story could not be true. She must have been in on the robbery.

Copper's Courage (page 70)—Because Junior was between Copper and the charging dogs, Copper apparently thought they were attacking Junior. Forgetting his usual fears, he instinctively reacted to protect his master.

One Foggy Night (page 24)—Dr. Quicksolve was afraid Officer Goodheart robbed the bank and made up his story to cover up after he wrecked the police car trying to get away with the money. Dr. Quicksolve knew that an experienced driver would not turn on his bright lights in the fog, and a suspect in the back of a police car would be locked in and unable to escape very easily.

The Thief's Glove (page 62)—Dr. Quicksolve was surprised when Terry said he found the "other glove" when he should not have known which glove (left or right) was used. The detective suspected Terry used Rod's glove to make it look like Rod was the thief.

Dark Suspicion (page 48)—The light came on inside the van. Since they watched it closely and it remained dark, they knew no one had opened that door and gotten out.

Pretty Rings in a Row (page 66)—Dr. Quicksolve knew that the only things that left the immediate premises were the tennis balls Jean-Luc hit over the fence. He may have slit a few tennis balls open and stuffed them with diamond rings, planning to hit them over the fence and retrieve them later.

Disappearing Duffel (page 36)—Junior thinks John Bigdood took his bag and quickly shoved it into his own football bag as he walked out of the locker room. Then he tossed his bag into the girls' locker room to hide it and look innocent when Junior came out into the hall.

Hideout (page 56)—Dr. Quicksolve knew Simon Smudge was too smart to start the boat's motor right away when he could paddle away silently and unseen in the dense fog. He also would have made sure the other boat would not be able to follow them. Dr. Quicksolve was right. Simon and his henchmen had quietly pushed their car away from the cottage and driven away. The agent at Dr. Quicksolve's car was found knocked out, and Benjamin Clayborn Blowhard was found tied and gagged alone in the motorboat.

The Late Cal Culator (page 64)—Dr. Quicksolve suspected Don killed his roommate. Don said he saw the body and immediately ran out of the house and did not return. But it was so dark Sergeant Shurshot had to turn on the light before she and Dr. Quicksolve saw the body. If his story were true, the light would be on.

Woof! Woof! Bang! Bang! (page 30)—Sergeant Shurshot suspected Barrie Scarrie and was talking about his picture on his driver's license. Scarrie said he heard the dog bark and two shots. If a stranger had broken in, the dog would have probably reacted to protect his owner and their home. The dog would have been shot first. If a friend, like Scarrie, had been let in, the dog would not have barked until he saw his owner was hurt. Scarrie looked like a serious suspect.

Rat Cliff—Cain Is Slain (page 80)—The name "Iceman" was a constant clue to each murder which involved the use of ice. Dr. Quicksolve suspected Cain hired the Iceman to kill Abel and Birch. Then the Iceman killed Cain, the only one who knew he did it. He and Cain plotted to dump the car over the cliff and escape in a getaway car. The Iceman pretended to put a rock in front of the tire of the car and somehow convinced Cain to go back into the car. The rock was a block of ice that melted and sent the car plunging down the mountain with Cain still in it after the Iceman had coolly walked away.

B.B. Bigstuff (page 34)—Bluntnose could have shot B.B. the first time he was there by using a .22 with a silencer. He could then have left and gotten rid of the .22. After returning, he could have shot his .38 twice, out the window or with blanks, and quickly replaced one of the bullets in his .38 to make it look as if he had just fired one of the shots heard by the secretary.

Rat Cliff—One Down (page 76)—Dr. Quicksolve suspected the hair dryer and a block or pile of ice were placed on the bathroom floor while Abel was in the shower. The hair dryer, unheard because of the shower and vent fan, would melt the ice and provide the electricity for the deadly puddle Abel would step into when he stepped out of the shower. He suspected Cain was involved because he had removed himself the farthest from the situation.

Pie (page 12)—Junior knew that the kitchen floor was mopped just before they went to bed. He also knew that footprints were just as individual as fingerprints, even between twins.

Index

• • • • • • • • •